One Cup at a Time

Recipes for Recovery

Edited by Marilyn R. Gardner and Elizabeth Trotter

Acknowledgements

This project is a joint effort between the Community Advisory Board at Stanley Street Treatment and Resources, Inc., a global leader in addiction treatment and healthcare, and the Center for Health Impact.

We would like to thank Amy Dasilva, Caridad Diaz, Jaison Diaz, Leanne McCarthy, Paul Mendes, Martha Mendonca, Billie Jo Simmons, and Lamar Stevens. Each person has committed time and energy to being an active member of the Community Advisory Board at SSTAR Care Community Partners. As members, they offer valuable and hard-earned knowledge and experience to help SSTAR better understand the recovery process and community needs or gaps in service. Many of them have included recipes in this cookbook. In addition, Care Coordinators from the Behavioral Health Division at SSTAR have also contributed stories and recipes. The Care Coordinators know what it is to walk the long road of recovery with a person, encouraging them along the way. Special thanks to Kayla Green of SSTAR for working tirelessly to develop the Community Advisory Board. Her ongoing work is a gift to the community.

Center for Health Impact | centerforhealthimpact.org
SSTAR Addiction Treatment | sstar.org

First published 2022 by Doorlight Publications.

ISBN   0-9982233-6-0
ISBN13   978-0-9982233-6-0

Cover & Interior Design by Ruth Anne Burke

Contents

Introduction

One Cup at a Time: Recipes for Recovery is a community project that focuses on food, community, and recovery. Through these recipes and stories, we want to take you on a journey – a journey that is not a single story, but a collection of lives and experiences, of food and family, of resilience and recovery. Through stories we will explore the courage it takes to move into recovery; through food we will savor the tastes and traditions that honor each person's journey.

Cooking is not about one ingredient or one recipe. It's about a series of steps: a cup of this, a teaspoon of that, stir this, and mix that. It takes time, thought, and care. Just as in cooking, recovery does not have only one recipe for success. Instead, recovery is about taking one step at a time. It is a journey that takes many paths and turns. By sharing recipes that are meaningful to them, each contributor has given a window into their own journey and what it means to leave addictions behind and press on to a future marked by healthy relationships and sobriety.

We invite you to the project. Read. Taste. Savor. And through it, become one who can walk alongside those in recovery.

"Pull up a chair. Take a taste. Come join us. Life is so endlessly delicious."

Ruth Reichl

What is Recovery?

A dictionary definition of recovery tells us that it is a noun and refers to "a return to a normal state of health, mind, or strength." This definition feels too simple for what recovery means and for all that goes into someone's move from sobriety to recovery.

SAMSHA (the Substance Abuse and Mental Health Services Administration) identifies these ten guiding principles for recovery:

Emerges from hope
Is person-driven
Occurs through many pathways
Is holistic
Is supported by peers and allies
Is supported through relationships and social networks
Is culturally based and influenced
Is supported by addressing trauma
Involves individual, family, and community strengths and responsibility
Is based on respect

Just as cooking includes a variety of ingredients to create a delicious cake, bread, salad, or entrée, so it is with recovery. Recovery takes far more than one ingredient to be successful.

Since 1977, SSTAR has been committed to serving Fall River and the surrounding area with understanding, help, support, and hope to those in need, whether they struggle with an addiction or mental health need. Its mission is "to provide a quality continuum of care and support to all people, especially those affected by addiction, by responding to their mental, physical, emotional, and spiritual needs."

SSTAR's values include:

Tradition: To preserve our heritage of providing services tailored to those who are addicted and affected by addiction.

Leadership: To set the standard in the community regarding the education, prevention, and treatment of addiction.

Teamwork: To design and provide services in a non-judgmental, respectful, and culturally competent manner, enabling the greatest level of partnership and self-determination for each consumer.

Accountability: To deliver this care so that it is accessible, affordable, effective, and efficient.

Respect: To care for individuals regardless of their circumstances and to treat consumers and their families, as well as our employees and colleagues, with dignity and honesty.

Learning: To improve our understanding of disease, trauma, and social stigma.

Harm Reduction: To facilitate services appropriate to the circumstances, needs, and wishes of the consumer.

Expertise: To share our knowledge regarding the provision of health care and social services to those disenfranchised from traditional services. This knowledge base includes the dynamics and treatment of addiction, women's issues, HIV/AIDS, trauma, as well as primary and preventative medical care.

"I would rather go through life sober, believing that I'm an alcoholic, than go through life drunk, trying to convince myself that I am not."

Anonymous

Cooking as a Recovery Activity

Cooking can be a tremendous recovery activity. It has the potential to challenge you in new ways and to build up confidence in a new skill. Cooking can be a connector to others, where healthy friendships are made through sharing recipes and meals. The American Addiction Centers offer four ways that cooking can be beneficial to recovery.

Physical Health It is easy to ignore your eating habits and physical health when you are in the midst of addiction. As you move into recovery, being aware of what you are eating by taking the time to cook is a great way to better your physical health.

Brain Following a recipe, choosing ingredients, and working with kitchen tools are all ways to increase your cognitive skills. As you cook, you will increase your attention span and ability to concentrate. Start with simple meals, and as you gain confidence, you can make meals that are more complex.

Mental Health Our eating habits don't just affect our physical health. They also affect our mental health. High sugar content, junk food, and processed foods don't help us to feel our best. As you prepare meals, you can think about the way the fresh ingredients will help your body and your mind.

Friendship Recovery cannot happen in isolation. We need people to come beside us. Cooking is a way to build connections with friends and family. The act of putting a meal together takes teamwork and creativity and reminds us that we are not alone.

About the Community Advisory Board

The SSTAR Care Community Partners program is proud to be in partnership with our Community Advisory Board, which serves as a voice for our member population and the greater community. We come together to discover each other's perspectives, discuss needs, assets, and barriers, focus on solutions, and identify ways to improve and best serve our community. We also have a bit of fun along the way! It has been a rewarding experience for the organization and board members alike. The board is comprised of members from diverse backgrounds and life experiences. These experiences include both struggles and triumphs in the lifelong process that is recovery.

Kayla Green

Community Liaison to the Community Advisory Board and
Care Coordinator at SSTAR Care Community Partners

"Recovery, to me, is like life. You just try to better yourself, and no matter how hard it gets, remember to look to your loved ones. They will push you to not give up and always love yourself, have faith, and thank God for another day."

Caridad Diaz

Main Courses

"If the home is a body, the table is the heart, the beating center, the sustainer of life and health."

Shauna Niequist

Garden Tomato Sauce
Harvard Thompson

The next two recipes are for and from my family. While they are my own creation, they were made for family members, who have been instrumental in my culinary and agricultural introductions. We start with the plants: sowing seeds, nurturing them, and learning the perfect time to harvest the fruits of our labor takes time and patience (both of which my family has been generous to afford me). Next comes the kitchen experience, which is all about bringing the raw ingredients to life and drawing out the innate sweetness that they all offer. Tomatoes, if grown with enough love (which really means proper soil pH balance, irrigation, weeding, pruning, and of course, talking to them), will be so sweet that you don't need to add sugar to the recipe. Then we learn how to blend flavors together, incorporating the right balance of the Italian trifecta (i.e., olive oil, garlic, and Parmesan cheese). Trial and error is expected. The best proof of success is when your relatives return the casserole dishes to you empty and with a request for a refill!

This is my personal tomato sauce recipe, which I have been making every year I have had a vegetable garden. The purpose is to not let a single tomato go to waste. Add peppers and eggplants, along with herbs from the garden to make it more robust (though this is not required). The secret ingredient for this sauce is the grated carrots. They reduce the acidity of the tomatoes, add sweetness, and thicken the sauce so that it resembles a meat sauce.

Ingredients

2-5 lbs of fresh tomatoes, or 2 large cans diced plus 2 large cans pureed tomatoes

4-6 cloves of garlic, finely chopped

6-10 mushrooms, sliced

2-4 peppers (bell or cubanello), diced

4-6 carrots, grated

2-4 Tbsp of olive oil

2-3 bay leaves, whole

salt and pepper to taste

optional: red pepper flakes to taste (for heat)

Directions

Place the tomatoes, oil, garlic, and spices in a big pot. Bring to a boil, then reduce heat to medium, stirring every 10 minutes.

Once the tomatoes begin to break down, add the mushrooms, peppers, and carrots.

Simmer on low for 1 hour.

Before serving, remember to remove the bay leaves.

Turkey Meatballs
Harvard Thompson

This is a trusted recipe that I have made for every family member and friend who was ever in need of a home-cooked meal made with love.

Ingredients

1 ¼ lb package of 80% lean turkey, shredded

1 medium Vidalia onion, chopped extra fine

1 clove of garlic, chopped fine

Italian-flavored breadcrumbs (exact measure depends on the moisture/consistency of the mix)

1 egg

dash of salt

dash of pepper

Italian seasoning

Parmesan cheese (grated)

Directions

In a mixing bowl, combine all the ingredients. Use your (well-washed) hands to mix. Add breadcrumbs a little at a time to make the mix less wet, if needed. You know you've reached the optimal consistency of the mix when it sticks to itself but not to the bowl or your fingers. Be careful not to make it too dry.

Form the mixture into small balls by rolling them between your hands. Try to keep the size of the meatballs consistent.

Brown the meatballs in a pan with olive oil (rotating to get all sides cooked).

Add the cooked meatballs to the Garden Tomato Sauce, place sauce on low, and cook for 1.5 hours.

Serve over pasta.

"Healthy" One-Pan Hamburger Helper
(Cheesy Italian Shells)
Kylie Brewer

The story with this recipe is less heartwarming and more heart protecting. When I was growing up, boxed meals like Hamburger Helper were always a go-to for my parents for dinner. They had a big family, and it was hard to feed four kids and themselves on a budget, so meals with pasta and ground beef were common. When I moved out, I found myself wanting to make this comfort food but was honestly not a big fan of the long list of added ingredients, preservatives, and salt in those prepackaged boxes. I decided to try making my own from ingredients around the house and ended up with this awesome meal that can easily feed a family of six.

Ingredients

1 lb ground beef

1 box of pasta shells

1 can of plain tomato soup

2 cups of low-fat shredded cheddar cheese

1 ½ cups beef or chicken broth

1 cup skim milk

1 Tbsp Italian seasoning mix

1 tsp black pepper

1 tsp salt

1 tsp paprika

½ tsp red pepper flakes

Directions

In a large skillet (one with deep sides) over medium-high heat, brown the ground beef and break it apart as it cooks.

Drain the fat out into a separate container, and dispose of it once it cools.

Return the beef to the burner and add spices, milk, and broth. Mix well.

Mix in the can of tomato soup and add the box of pasta. Make sure the pasta is covered by the liquid in the pan.

Bring to a boil, then reduce to a simmer (on low heat). Cover.

Stir every 5-10 minutes until the pasta is al dente, then shut off the heat.

Mix in the shredded cheese and serve!

Beef Stew
Kylie Brewer

Ingredients

1-2 lb stew meat
2 Tbsp olive oil
2 Tbsp flour
1 yellow onion, chopped
5 russet potatoes, peeled and
    chopped into 1-2 inch pieces
2 cups baby carrots
1 bag frozen peas
8-10 cups beef stock or broth
½ cup red wine (may substitute
    ¼ cup red wine vinegar or
    white vinegar)
Spices (season to taste):
1 tsp salt
1 tsp pepper
1 tsp red pepper flakes
2 tsp garlic powder
2 tsp onion powder
1 Tbsp thyme
½ Tbsp oregano
½ Tbsp rosemary
2 bay leaves

Directions

In a large stew pot or Dutch oven, heat the olive oil to brown the stew meat over medium-high heat. Sprinkle it with flour towards the end of cooking so that it combines with the fat and the meat.

Remove the meat from the pan.

Add the diced onion and garlic to the pan, and cook until you just begin to smell them.

Pour in the red wine or vinegar.

If using wine, allow to boil for 1-2 minutes on high heat, then add the stew meat back in. If using vingear, skip this step.

Add beef stock, carrots, potatoes, and all your desired seasonings.

Bring to a boil, and then reduce heat to low. Simmer 3-4 hours.

Serve with warm bread and butter.

To make in the slow cooker: Use some type of vinegar, NOT red wine. Follow steps 1 and 2, then add the meat to the slow cooker with the rest of the ingredients. Cook on low for 6-8 hours or on high for 4-6.

Slow Cooker Garlic Teriyaki Chicken
Kylie Brewer

Ingredients

6-8 boneless chicken thighs OR
   4-5 breasts

1 cup soy sauce

½ cup honey

pinches of salt and pepper

1 Tbsp garlic

2 Tbsp brown sugar

optional: 1 tsp crushed red
   pepper flakes

Directions

Combine soy sauce, honey, garlic, and brown sugar into a sauce.

Place the chicken in a single layer in a slow cooker, and season lightly with salt and pepper. Pour the sauce over the chicken.

Cook on low for 6 hours or high for 4 hours.

Serve over rice and vegetable(s) of choice (my favorite is carrots or broccoli!).

To cook in the oven: place the chicken in an oven-safe dish and cover with the prepared sauce. Bake at 375°F for about 30 minutes.

"Recovery didn't open the gates of heaven and let me in.
Recovery opened the gates of hell and let me out."

Anonymous

Lasagna with a "Puerto Rican Twist"

Pedro Cruz

This recipe is important to me because it reminds me of my days in Puerto Rico as a child. This became my go-to food every time I visited Grandma. I could not enjoy Grandma's lasagna from afar after moving to the States, so I decided to make and create my own lasagna recipe with a twist. This lasagna is to-die-for, and even my grandma is jealous.

This recipe can easily feed 9-12 depending on portion/serving size.

Ingredients

9 lasagna sheets

disposable lasagna pan (for an easy clean up)

1.5-2 lbs ground beef of choice (I prefer lean 93/7, but 80/20 also works)

2-3 oz of cream cheese

24-oz jar of tomato sauce (I prefer Traditional Prego)

shredded mozzarella cheese

1-2 Tbsp cooking oil of choice

2 Tbsp sofrito

½ Tbsp (or more) adobo

½ Tbsp garlic powder

sprinkle of oregano flakes

salt and pepper to taste

2 ripe plantains (peel your own or use Goya microwavable Ripe Plantains from the freezer section)

Directions

Preheat the oven to 350° F.

Start by boiling the lasagna sheets (follow the instructions of the pasta packaging). This can cook in the background, and once it is fully cooked, remove and strain.

On medium-high heat, add your cooking oil, just enough to coat the surface of the pan (about 2 Tbsp).

Add 2 Tbsp of sofrito and sauté for a minute or two until your home smells like paradise. Add ground beef and cook for about 5 minutes.

Add adobo to taste (start with ½ Tbsp and go from there), ½ Tbsp garlic powder, oregano flakes, and salt and pepper to taste. Stir to incorporate all the ingredients, then cover with a lid until fully cooked.

Once fully cooked, add about half of your tomato sauce into your meat and stir. Save the rest of your sauce for later.

Add the 2-3 ounces of cream cheese to the meat, and stir. At this point your lasagna meat is all set! It's time to assemble.

If you are peeling your own ripe plantains (the darker the better), peel and cut the two plantains into pieces and boil until soft, then strain and mash. Alternatively, you can just pop the freezer Goya plantains into the microwave.

Lay down 3 lasagna sheets in the lasagna pan, and lightly coat them in the leftover tomato sauce. Top with your mashed plantains, then add your meat, remembering to keep some for your second layer. Sprinkle with mozzarella cheese, and layer one is complete. Lay down another 3 pasta sheets and lightly coat with pasta sauce, add meat, sprinkle with mozzarella cheese, and layer two is complete. Lay down another 3 sheets, coat with the remainder of the pasta sauce, and cover the top layer with mozzarella.

Bake your lasagna until the cheese is melted, about 25-30 minutes depending on your oven.

Enchilada Casserole
Kimberly LePage

Ingredients

1 lb lean ground beef (90% lean)

1 large onion, chopped

2 cups salsa

1 can (15 ounces) black beans, rinsed and drained

1/4 cup Italian salad dressing

1 packet taco seasoning (or about 2 Tbsp)

6 flour tortillas (8 inches)

1 container reduced fat sour cream (16 oz)

1 packet shredded Mexican cheese blend (8 oz)

1 cup shredded lettuce

1 medium tomato, chopped

¼ cup minced fresh cilantro

Directions

Preheat the oven to 400° F.

In a large skillet, cook the beef and onion over medium heat until the meat is no longer pink; drain.

Stir in the salsa, beans, dressing, and taco seasoning. Coat a rectangular baking dish with cooking spray; place 3 tortillas on the bottom of the dish. Layer with half of the meat mixture, sour cream, and cheese. Repeat layers.

Cover and bake for 25 minutes. Uncover; bake until heated through, about 5-10 minutes longer. Let stand for 5 minutes; top with lettuce, tomato, and cilantro.

Lugaw
Janel Doloiras

Lugaw is basically Filipino Chicken Soup for the Soul! It's the go-to dish when you're sick or homesick. Depending on whether it's a real sickness, you can increase the amount of ginger, garlic, and veggies. It's a guarantee to make you feel better. Other cultures have something similar and may call it porridge, Congee, or Arroz Caldo. This is the basic recipe that I use, but because the recipes I've learned don't really have measurements, feel free to experiment!

Ingredients

butter

1 onion, chopped

1 handful of garlic, crushed

1 handful of ginger, thinly sliced
(or ½ -1 Tbsp pureed ginger)

2-4 douses of fish sauce (patis)

1 cup jasmine rice

5-6 chicken bouillon cubes

2-3 chicken thighs (optional)

Top with:

boiled egg(s), green onions,
the crispies from the fried
garlic, and calamansi (or
lemon/lime if you don't have
calamansi on hand)

salt and pepper or extra fish
sauce to taste

Directions

Melt some butter and sauté the onion, garlic, and ginger. Separate some crispier pieces of the garlic, if you can, to add for toppings later.

Add rice, fish sauce, bouillon cubes, and one cup of water for each bouillon cube you use.

Simmer while the rice soaks up the water and thickens, mixing every few minutes. This takes about 30 minutes.

Boil the egg(s) separately while the rice simmers. Depending on what you prefer, you can either soft boil or hard boil the eggs. Cook for 6 minutes for soft-boiled or 10 minutes for hard-boiled. When the time is up, place the egg in a bowl of ice water. Peel once it cools.

Serve the Lugaw topped with green onions, some crispy garlic, boiled egg(s), and calamansi (or lemon/lime). You can add fish sauce or salt and pepper to taste.

Variations:

Sometimes I like it with a thicker consistency, like porridge. For example, I feed it to my son as a porridge because at this consistency it's less of a mess when he tries to scoop it with a spoon. I usually make my "start batch" this thicker consistency, but when I eat it or make it for adults, I add more water so that it has more of a soupy consistency. If you add more water, you can also add another bouillon cube.

You can also add chicken. If you do, I'd recommend using chicken thighs. Cook the chicken in the same pan after sautéing the onions, garlic, and ginger. Then follow the rest of the steps once the chicken is almost done cooking. It will continue to cook while the rice simmers.

Fisherman's Shrimp Stuffing
Billie Jo Simmons

Steve died on December 14, 2003. He was lost at sea. Christmas was very tough for us that year — it was the saddest day ever, but we got through it. Then came New Year's. Every New Year Steve made his Baked Stuffed Shrimp, but this year we didn't even have the recipe. On New Year's Eve, I started going through his things to donate them, and wouldn't you know it, I found his recipe, in his handwriting, like a gift from heaven. I started crying and thanking him for showing me a sign that he's watching over us. That New Year's Eve I made Baked Stuffed Shrimp, and I've made it every New Year's for almost 20 years. I miss him every day.

Ingredients

jumbo shrimp

1 sleeve Ritz crackers

1 stick butter

1 can crab meat, drained

splash of lemon juice

Directions

Preheat oven to 350° F. Spray a large sheet pan with nonstick spray.

Crumble the Ritz crackers and melt the butter. Mix everything together with your hands until it is well blended.

Peel the shrimp without removing the tail. Insert a knife about three-quarters of the way into the shrimp near the head, and cut nearly all the way down the center of the shrimp's back to the tail. Remove the vein with the tip of your knife. Use your hands to open the shrimp until it lies flat. Rinse thoroughly.

Lay the butterflied shrimp on a baking sheet.

Press about a tablespoon of stuffing between your hands until it forms an egg-shaped ball, then press into the butterflied shrimp.

Bake for 30 minutes.

Canja
Billie Jo Simmons

Ingredients

2 cans chicken broth

12 chicken wings

1 large onion, chopped

5 spears celery, chopped

2 quarts water

5 bay leaves

2 Tbsp paprika

1 cup short-grain rice

Directions

Combine the water, chicken broth, bay leaves, celery, onion, paprika, salt, pepper, and chicken wings in a pot. Boil until the chicken is cooked. Add the rice and continue to simmer until the rice is cooked. Serve and enjoy!

"It's not that some people have will power and some don't. It's that some people are ready to change and others are not."

James Gordon

Bucaou - Salt Cod Stew

Billie Jo Simmons

Ingredients

5 pieces of salted cod (flaked and desalted)

5 medium potatoes, chopped, with skins on

4 onions

2 garlic cloves

3 boiled eggs, sliced

black olives

salt and pepper

olive oil

Directions

Boil cod for 10 minutes; cool and flake.

Use the cod water to boil the potatoes (remember to keep the skins on). Cool.

In a frying pan, sauté onions and garlic with ½ cup of olive oil. Remove from the heat.

In a baking dish, layer the potatoes and cod. Pour the onion, garlic, and oil over it. Salt and pepper to taste.

Bake for 30 minutes at 350°F; top with eggs and olives.

Muamba Chicken
James Figueiredo

I have achieved some fame among family and friends for my signature muamba dish. For around 30 years I have hosted an end-of-summer muamba party at my home in the Azores. Many memories are tied to this special dish as special friends gather to say farewell while eating this meal underneath the fig tree. I first made this dish nearly 30 years ago. My colleague, Ana Maria Morais, had shared her family recipe with me. This was many years before CNN declared it to be one of the ten most delicious foods in the world in 2011. While there are many ways to prepare this dish, I feel loyal to the way I first tasted it in Ana's kitchen.

Ingredients

1 large chicken, quartered	2 Tbsp of palm oil	1 lemon
1 fresh tomato, chopped	2 Tbsp of olive oil	1 ½ tsp of chili powder
½ head of minced garlic cloves	2 bay leaves	1 bunch of collard greens
2+ large onions, sliced	1 tsp salt	¼ lb of okra (optional)
¾ cup of chunky peanut butter without added sugar	2+ hot chili peppers (to taste)	6 servings of yucca, rice, or cornmeal mash as desired

Directions

Combine lemon juice, minced garlic, salt, chili powder; rub all over chicken and allow to marinate for at least one hour (preferably overnight).

Heat the palm oil and olive oil in a pot over medium heat, and brown the chicken on all sides.

Add the onion, chopped tomato, and the remaining marinade; bring to a boil. Cover, reduce heat, and simmer until the chicken is tender, about one hour. Add strips of collard greens, and cook until tender.

Serve over boiled yucca, rice, or cornmeal mash.

Spanish Chicken Stew
Caridad Diaz

From the age of ten I've been cooking. My mom always taught me, "Cook with your heart! Cook with love."

Ingredients

10 pieces of boneless chicken thighs	1 spoon of sofrito if you have it (if not it's OK)
1 box of chicken broth	garlic powder
½ cup or more of cooking white wine	onion powder
2 cans of tomato sauce	paprika
2 packets of sazon (coriander & annatto)	parsley flakes
1 packet of chicken-flavored bouillon powder	adobo con sazon
1 packet of ham-flavored bouillon powder	cilantro leaves

Directions

In a large stew pot or Dutch oven, sear the chicken. Once the chicken is golden, remove it from the pan and set it aside (it does not need to be cooked through yet).

In the same pot, combine the rest of the ingredients.

Simmer for 1-2 minutes.

Add the chicken back to the pot. Bring it to a boil and then turn the heat to low. Cover and simmer for about 30 minutes. Then uncover and cook the stew for another 10-15 minutes on medium-high heat to reduce the sauce.

Jag
Martha Mendonca

Jag is short for Jagacida and is an adapted recipe for Cape Verdean Beans and Rice. This recipe has been on tables in the Southeast Region of Massachusetts for many years. Like the best recipes, Jag is usually passed down through the family, and each family has a slightly different variation of this household staple. The online website, *Edible Southshore*, says this: "a few early twentieth-century Yankee cookbooks do contain recipes for 'jagasee' and, interestingly, do not refer to it as anything terribly exotic. In the absence of hard documentation, it's fun to contemplate how a West African staple became a part of the supposedly closed diet of Anglo New Englanders—possibly a testament to the power of good food and shared hard work on land or sea."[1]

Ingredients	Directions
1 Tbsp oil	Heat 1 Tbsp of oil in a pot.
linguica sausage	Sauté the linguica until lightly browned.
onion	Add the onion and cook until it is soft and translucent.
2 packages sazon	Add the water, sazon, and kidney beans. Bring it to a boil.
kidney beans	Add the rice and reduce the heat to low. Let it simmer until all the water is absorbed, about 25 minutes.
2 cups rice	
4 cups water	

---

1   https://ediblesouthshore.com/recipes/entrees/jagacida/

Soups and Side Dishes

"If you're afraid of butter, use cream."

Julia Child

Cream of Poblano Soup
Fred Rocco

This recipe is for my own version of cream of poblano soup. I first tasted this soup in Mexico at a small restaurant. In my (terrible) Spanish I tried to get the recipe and got some story about having to come back on Wednesdays when the cook was in (at least that's what I could gather in my attempts to communicate). Needless to say, I never got the recipe, but I determined to make it at home, nonetheless. Several earlier attempts at this soup went down the garbage disposal. This recipe is my best approximation, because I never write anything down . . . so feel free to vary the amounts.

Ingredients

fresh poblano peppers (at least 8)

1 onion

garlic (several cloves)

fresh cilantro

Goya Recaito Culantro cooking base

chicken or vegetable broth

olive oil

half and half or whole milk

4-5 jalepeno peppers

adobo seasoning

the juice from about 2 limes

celery (1-2 stalks)

other spices if you want

Directions

Cut the peppers in half and take out the seeds. Cut the celery and onion into about 2-3 inch pieces.

Coat the peppers, celery, onion, and garlic with olive oil.

Roast the vegetables on a grill or in your oven until they start to blacken.

If you want, you can take the time to remove the blackened skin from the peppers, but you don't have to.

Purée all the grilled vegetables and a few tablespoons of broth in a food processor.

Place the puréed ingredients in a large pot and simmer on low heat. Add one to two jars of Goya Recaito. Let simmer for about 30-40 minutes; you can add water or broth as it cooks to keep it the right consistency.

Chop the cilantro and add to the soup. Add some adobo (to taste), along with salt and pepper. If you want to kick up the heat, feel free to add hotter spices like cayenne. Squeeze in the lime juice as well. Towards the end of cooking, add half and half or whole milk until you have the consistency of a creamy soup.

And that's it. You can vary the vegetables — feel free to roast a potato or tomato and throw it in the mix.

Buffalo Chicken Dip
Amy DaSilva

Ingredients

2 boneless chicken breasts (you can use 2 10-ounce cans of chunk chicken if you're in a rush)

¾ cup hot sauce (I use Frank's RedHot, but you can use whatever hot sauce your family prefers)

2 16-ounce packages of cream cheese

1 cup of ranch dressing

1 ½ cups of mild cheddar cheese

crackers and/or Tostitos for dipping

celery (optional)

Directions

Preheat the oven to 275°F and soften the cream cheese.

Cook and shred the chicken very well. I have used 2 forks, and I have also used a blender on low. (Skip this step if using the cans, but make sure to drain them.)

Once the chicken is all shredded, put it into a skillet with the hot sauce and mix, cooking on medium until it is heated thoroughly.

Pour in the ranch dressing and softened cream cheese and mix well (keep on medium heat).

Once the cream cheese is melted, pour in half the cheddar cheese and mix until it's all slightly bubbling.

Pour your buffalo dip into a pan. (My round cake pan or pie pan works best and fits everything perfectly.) Sprinkle the rest of the cheddar cheese on top and bake on the low oven setting until your edges are bubbling (usually about 30-40 minutes).

Serve with your choice of crackers or celery (or both). I think Chicken in a Biskit crackers go especially well with this dip.

"Recovery is like fighting a devil every day and winning. I love the feeling of being the champion every single day."

Amy DaSilva

Escarole and Beans in Oil

Harvard Thompson

Ingredients

2 large heads escarole, chopped

2 cans cannellini beans (or 1 package dried, which will need to be soaked overnight to rehydrate)

2 large Vidalia or yellow onions, chopped

4 cloves garlic, chopped

1 can black olives

1 ½ cups mixed herbs (rosemary, parsley, basil, thyme), chopped

salt

pepper

lemon pepper

Old Bay seasoning

1 Tbsp chicken or vegetable stock

Parmesan cheese

Directions

Blanch escarole in salted water in a large pot. Drain, reserving 1-2 cups of water.

In a large saucepan, add olive oil, onions, olives, garlic, chicken or vegetable stock, and herbs. Sauté until crunchy.

Add the escarole and reserved water; cook until crunchy.

Add the beans and heat the mixture, then add the spices. The flavors should begin to meld.

Serve warm with olive oil drizzled on top, and with some Parmesan cheese.

Baccala and Artichoke
Harvard Thompson

Ingredients

baccala (salted cod) — portion according to the desired number of mouths to feed

olive oil

lemon

2-3 cloves garlic

1 cup white wine

salt

pepper

1 can crushed tomatoes

1 medium Vidalia or yellow onion, chopped

mushrooms, sliced

parsley, chopped

1 can artichoke wedges

Parmesan cheese

Directions

Soak the baccala for 48 hours prior to cooking. Change the water 5 times to make sure you remove all the salt.

Sauté garlic in olive oil until golden.

Place the fish in the pan, skin side down.

Add white wine and pepper, then cover and simmer for 15 minutes (until the fish flakes).

Turn off the heat, remove the fish from the pan, and set aside.

Keep the juices in the pan and add crushed tomatoes, chopped onions, more garlic, and mushrooms. Simmer for 5-10 minutes.

When the mushrooms and onions are cooked, take the pan off of the heat.

Add artichoke wedges, parsley, and lemon juice.

Plate the fish and pour the sauce on top.

Garnish with additional parsley, Parmesan cheese, and salt and pepper.

Fattoush Salad
Marilyn Gardner

Fattoush is a Lebanese salad that I was introduced to while living in Egypt. Our favorite Lebanese restaurant served up large bowls of the salad at outside cafe tables. We would sit and eat the salad along with fresh lemon mint smoothies. When I moved to the United States, I missed this salad and worked to adapt it from my memory. It is a refreshing summer salad with pungent, mouth-watering Middle Eastern flavors. The key ingredient is sumac, a deep red spice with citrusy flavor and a tart taste. It is used in many Iranian and Middle Eastern recipes. Sumac can be purchased at Middle Eastern grocery stores or online.

Ingredients

1 head romaine lettuce

3 large tomatoes

1 large red onion

3-4 Persian cucumbers

6-8 mint leaves

large handful of cilantro

salt and pepper to taste

sumac spice

1 cup of crispy pita chips, broken into bite-size pieces

Dressing:

⅓ cup olive oil

¼ - ⅓ cup lemon juice

Directions

Chop all the ingredients (except pita chips) into bite-size pieces. Mix everything together, and add salt, pepper, and sumac spice. Refrigerate until you're ready to serve. Add the pita chips and dressing right before serving.

Carrots and Turnips
Kayla Green

This is a dish that signifies the joining of families and traditions. My partner and I have been together for nearly seven years, and we share a daughter together. For the first few years, neither of us really contributed to Thanksgiving as far as cooking, and we would alternate whose mom's house we went to each year. Then I decided that I wanted to do an entire Thanksgiving dinner by myself. The only food that my partner asked for was this simple carrots and turnips dish because it was a staple at his family's Thanksgiving table since childhood. Since then, no matter where we eat for Thanksgiving, I make this dish for him. It is always a conversation starter for my side of the family, as it is something that we never made.

Ingredients

some carrots

some turnips

butter

salt and pepper

Directions

Boil carrots and turnips, either together or separately, until soft. Mash them together with butter and seasonings to taste (I use salt and pepper).

"Recovery is an acceptance that your life is in shambles and you have to change it."

Jamie Lee Curtis

Poblanos Rellenos
Gloria Acosta

Ingredients

6 poblano peppers, cut lengthwise and seeded

1 lb gound beef or ground vegan meat

1 Tbsp olive oil

1 onion, chopped

2 garlic cloves, minced

1 zucchini, cut into small pieces

1 cup cooked black beans

½ cup cooked brown rice

1 cup salsa verde

1 Tbsp taco seasoning (chili powder, cumin, red pepper flakes, pepper, cayenne)

salt to taste

1 cup shredded Mexican cheese blend

red pepper flakes

Directions

Preheat the oven to 375°F.

Roast the peppers on an oiled tray for 15 minutes.

Sauté the onions, garlic, ground meat, and zucchini. Season with taco seasoning, adding salt to taste.

Once cooked, add the black beans and rice.

Mix in the salsa verde.

Put the filling in the roasted poblanos. Sprinkle with cheese and red pepper flakes.

Place in the oven until the cheese is melted and starting to bubble.

Enjoy!

Sweets

"Cakes are healthy too, you just eat a small slice."

Mary Berry

An Uncommon Carrot Cake

Marilyn Gardner

By the time she was 21, my mother-in-law had her hands full with four little boys. When my husband was very young, but old enough to remember, his mom said to all of them: "Pick your birthday cake and stick with it." They did! From then on, each of them knew that every year their favorite cake would emerge on their birthday. My husband picked carrot cake. I learned this in our first year of marriage, and now, 37 years later, a 9 inch by 11 inch pan of goodness appears before him every birthday. It is uncommonly delicious! The day I make it, the whole house smells like a mixture of cinnamon and sweetness as it bakes in the oven.

Ingredients

1 bag grated carrots	¾ cup walnuts	**For icing:**
3 eggs	2 cups flour	8 oz cream cheese
1 cup light brown sugar	1 tsp baking powder	½ cup butter
½ cup white sugar	2 tsp baking soda	3 cups icing sugar
1 cup oil	2 tsp cinnamon	1 tsp vanilla
1 cup coconut	1 tsp allspice	
1 cup crushed pineapple	2 tsp vanilla	

Directions

Preheat the oven to 350ºF. Grease and flour a 9x11 inch pan.

Put the carrots in a saucepan with ¼ cup of water. Cook until they are semi-soft. Put in a food processor or equivalent and add some of the pineapple juice. Blend and set aside.

Beat the eggs until they are light and fluffy. Add both brown and white sugars and continue beating. Add the oil and beat until blended. Add the cinnamon, allspice, vanilla, baking powder, and baking soda. Add 2 cups of flour and blend until smooth.

Then add mashed carrots, coconut, pineapple, and walnuts. The mixture will be dense. Pour it into a greased and floured 9x11 inch pan.

Bake for about 45-50 minutes.

Cool completely and frost with cream cheese icing.

To make your own icing, mix 8 oz of softened cream cheese, ½ cup of softened butter, 3 cups icing sugar, and 1 tsp vanilla until it's smooth.

No-Fail Peanut Butter Fudge
Marilyn Gardner

Every time I come across this handwritten recipe, I pause. It is from my cousin Kristine and written long ago when I was getting married. My mom gathered family recipes, and this is the one that she sent in. Kristine died too young on January 27, 2007 – it was my 47th birthday. She was only 2 years older than me. I always stop and think about the two children she left behind, now adults. I wonder if her family remembers this No-Fail Peanut Butter Fudge, its sweet goodness a distant memory. I think of her mom, my Aunt Ruth who died this past year — one of the smartest, loveliest women on the planet — and I wonder if she had passed on the recipe to Kristine. I will never know, but just having the recipe and passing it on feels like a tribute to Kristine, to my Aunt Ruth, and to the abiding power of family and the recipes that get passed on.

Ingredients

2 cups sugar

2 Tbsp butter

1 cup milk

1 tsp vanilla

dash of salt

¾ cup peanut butter

Directions

Boil the sugar, milk, and salt for 10 minutes. Add the butter.

Continue boiling until mixture forms a soft ball in cold water (1-2 minutes).

Remove from the heat.

Add vanilla and peanut butter. Beat until the mixture starts to set.

Pour quickly into a buttered 8x8 inch square pan. Let cool and cut into squares.

Best Blondies
Marilyn Gardner

This recipe is a tried and true, quick delight! If you need something deliciously sweet and easy, this is the recipe for you.

Ingredients

½ cup butter

1 cup packed brown sugar

1 egg

1 tsp vanilla

¼ tsp almond extract

1 cup flour

½ tsp baking powder

⅛ tsp baking soda

⅓ cup chopped walnuts

½ cup chocolate chips

Directions

Preheat the oven to 350°F.

Melt the butter in a saucepan. Add the brown sugar and whisk until smooth. Add vanilla, almond extract, and egg and whisk again until smooth.

Mix in dry ingredients and chopped walnuts and pour into greased 8x8 inch pan. Sprinkle chocolate chips on top of the batter.

Bake for 22 minutes. Blondies will look set but soft.

Cool and cut into squares. Serve plain or with vanilla ice cream.

Nana's Pizzelle Recipe
Allison Marrier

This recipe is for a classic Italian cookie that we make every year for the holiday season. At my wedding a platter of these cookies lay on every table, handmade by my nana herself! For this recipe you need a special pizzelle press that can be purchased from all major retailers online. You won't regret adding this delicious treat to your holiday table. My nana would be proud of the addition!

Ingredients

3 eggs, beaten

¾ cup sugar

¾ cup butter, melted

1 ½ - 2 cups of flour

1 tsp baking powder

2 tsp vanilla

1 tsp anise extract (optional)

powdered sugar (for dusting the cookies at the end)

Directions

Combine and beat ingredients together in the order listed, except for the powdered sugar. Set the powdered sugar aside until the end. For thinner pizzelles, use the smaller amount of flour.

Drop a rounded spoonful of batter onto the center of the preheated pizzelle press. Close the lid immediately and close the handle with clip. Allow the pizzelle to cook until it stops steaming (about 30 seconds). Remove with fork.

Lay the pizzelles flat on wire racks or towels and let cool. (While they are hot, they can be rolled into cylinder or cone shapes – Did someone say pizzelle cannoli? Pizzelle ice cream cone? Yum!)

Dust with powdered sugar and store in an airtight container.

"I only understood myself after I destroyed myself, and only in the process of fixing myself, did I know who I really was."

Anonymous

Biscoitos
(Portuguese Tea Biscuits)
Katelynn Sousa

I grew up with a vovó (grandmother) who made the best Portuguese desserts. I remember when she used to make malasadas (fried dough) – it was an all-day process. I would watch her "put the dough to sleep." She would put the dough in a steel pan and wrap it with so many blankets! She used to unwrap the blankets after a few hours to see if it had risen, and we had to whisper when talking near the dough so that we wouldn't wake it up. I remember that vividly. My vovó was a nurturing person. Whenever she made malasadas, everyone would gather. I never remember her being alone when making malasadas, that's how good of a baker she was! Every time I bake Portuguese desserts, it reminds me of her. I bake desserts when I need to reconnect. Unfortunately, this recipe won't be malasadas. I have not made malasadas since she passed in 2007, as no others compare.

In 2017 I went to São Miguel for the first time. In the village where I stayed, a bread truck would come through the village around 5 a.m. to deliver warm bread and freshly made biscoitos. You could purchase a huge bag of biscoitos from the truck! It was an experience I will never forget. I'm going to show you how to make Portuguese Tea Biscuits, also known as "Biscoitos." Whenever I make this recipe, I receive so many compliments! And when I make biscoitos, it brings me back to the times when I used to watch my vovó bake. I'm happy to share this recipe with you, and I hope that it brings you and your loved ones together. Now let's start baking!

Ingredients	Directions
1 stick of butter, melted	Preheat your oven to 350°F. Prep a cookie sheet with nonstick spray.
1 cup of sugar	First melt the butter (I usually microwave it for 15 seconds). If the butter isn't fully melted, that's ok, just stir it until it is! Let the butter cool a bit. Mix the butter and sugar together. After the butter and sugar is combined, add the 3 eggs and mix with a whisk or wooden spoon.
3 eggs, beaten	
3 cups of all-purpose flour	
2 tsp of baking powder	In a separate bowl, mix the flour and 2 tsp of baking powder. Then add the butter, sugar, and egg mixture.

Once the dough starts to form, you can use your hands to roll the dough into a log. If the dough is too sticky, you may need to add a sprinkle of flour.

Now comes the fun part! Scoop out a tablespoon worth of dough. You can roll the dough into a snake-like shape that's about 5 inches long and a ½ inch wide — this does not have to be perfect at all! Then make a circle with the dough, overlap the ends, and pinch the ends together. Depending on how big you make them, this recipe usually makes around 20 biscoitos. You can also roll the dough flat to about ¼ inch thick and use cookie cutters.

Once you have all of your biscoitos formed, placed them on the baking sheet. I usually whisk an egg and brush the tops of the biscoitos with it. This will make them nice and golden! Now put them in the oven for about 17-20 minutes. They should be a golden color. Remove them from the oven and put them on a cooling rack.

Once they are cooled to your liking, enjoy them with some tea or coffee. You can store them in an airtight container for up to 1 week, but they probably won't last that long since they are so yummy!

Banana Pudding Cookies
Tanisha Williams

I have many great recipes that my family loves. I always loved cooking, but I never thought I would enjoy baking. I was wrong about that! It all began when my husband asked if I could make banana bread. I was a little scared as I had never baked anything before. Well, I would make cookies from store-bought dough and place them in the oven, but I'd never made anything from scratch. Now I love baking – everything from banana bread filled with cream cheese, to s'mores bars, to pumpkin banana bread, rice pudding, hot cocoa bombs, and much, much more. The list goes on and on. One of my family's favorites is banana pudding cookies with white chocolate chips, which is also a win because it's so easy!

Ingredients

12 Tbsp of butter

¾ cup of light brown sugar

¼ cup of granulated sugar

1 box of banana pudding dry mix

2 large eggs

1 tsp of vanilla

1 tsp of baking soda

2 ¼ cups of flour

1 ¼ cups of white chocolate chips (I tend to use more)

Directions

Preheat oven to 350°F.

Combine the flour and baking soda in a medium-size bowl and set aside.

In another bowl mix the butter and sugars. (I always try to melt butter slightly in the microwave, as it makes it easier to mix with the sugars.)

Add the pudding mix and stir until well-blended.

Add in the eggs and vanilla and mix until smooth.

Combine the wet and dry mixtures. Once mixed add in the white chocolate chips.

Roll into balls and place on a parchment paper-lined baking sheet.

Bake for 8-9 minutes, and you are done!

They will look slightly undercooked. No worries, just let them sit and cool off, then enjoy!

Taunton High School Wheat Bars
Laura Branco

My family would make these during the holidays. Little did I know that once I entered Taunton High, I would be baking these in Home Economics Class. Wheat Bars were very popular in high school. They were made in class and served during lunches for a small fee. I want to say 50 cents for a big square wheat bar.

Our local grocery store also makes and sells them. I want to say it's a "Taunton thing," but I'm not sure if other towns and people make them too.

Wheat bars may sound healthy with the word "wheat" in the title, but if you look at the ingredients, there is quite a lot of butter and sugar, along with a thick layer of chocolate. However, they are delicious and so easy to make.

Ingredients

4 sticks butter

1 cup brown sugar

1 cup granulated sugar

2 eggs

2 ½ cups all-purpose flour

2 ½ cups rolled oats

For the Topping:

16 oz chocolate chips

1 stick butter

Directions

Preheat the oven to 350°F.

For the bars:

Soften the butter. Beat together the first 3 ingredients.

Beat the eggs seperately. Add the flour and oats to the eggs.

Combine all ingredients.

Bake 20-25 minutes in a 12x16 inch pan, or two smaller pans.

Cool completely; then add topping.

For chocolate topping:

Melt 16 oz of chocolate chips with 1 stick of butter. Spread onto the bars when they are fully cooled.

Oreo Balls

Kayla Green

I began making Oreo Balls after a close friend took me to a flea market where they were sold. I tried one and told her, "I can totally make these for you." A year has passed since then, and I have made countless batches of these because everyone loves them! They are a labor of love, as making just one batch took me almost two hours on the first attempt (although now with practice I can do it in about forty-five minutes). Being in the kitchen is a healthy coping skill for me, so I don't mind the time it takes at all. People have suggested that I begin selling them, but it is truly an expression of love for me, so I always give them as gifts.

Ingredients

1 package of Oreos (cannot be double stuffed, but any flavor is fine)

1 8-ounce package of cream cheese (softened is best)

dipping chocolate of any variety

candy toppings (optional)

Directions

Crush Oreos either in a food processor or by hand by putting the Oreos in a bag and mashing them up.

Mix cream cheese and crushed Oreos together.

Roll mixture into about 1-2 inch round balls and place on a baking sheet lined with parchment paper.

Put the tray into the freezer for at least 15 minutes.

Melt the dipping chocolate. Coat each ball completely and then return it to the tray.

Decorate with any kind of candy, sprinkles, etc.

Put back in the freezer for at least 15 minutes.

These can be stored in the freezer for up to two months!

Sinfully Rich Fudgy Brownies

Susan Worthen

One snowy day in Boston I saw this wonderful cookie book. I thought to myself, "I can make great cookies with my daughter forever with this book," so I bought it. She was six years old. That year we baked these wonderful fudgy brownies, and Ginger-Lee took them to Meeting Street School in East Providence, RI, to share with her classmates, teachers, PT, OT, and Speech Therapist. They were a huge hit. I also gave some to my sisters. The next year Ginger's teachers asked her if she and her mom were making those Fudgy Brownies again. She said, "I will have to ask my mommy." That year we bought cookie tins from Zayre's, made many dozens of small, bite-size morsels, and it all started. Happy Baking to everyone!

Ingredients

For the Brownies:

4 oz unsweetend chocolate
1 cup butter
4 eggs
2 cups sugar
1 Tbsp vanilla extract
¼ tsp salt
1 cup flour

For the Chocolate Marshmallow Frosting:

4 oz unsweetened chocolate
1 cup butter
2 eggs
1 Tbsp vanilla extract
1-lb package powdered sugar (3 ¾ cups)
4 cups mini marshmallows

Directions

Preheat oven to 350°F. Grease a 9x13 inch baking pan.

In a large saucepan, combine chocolate and butter. Heat over low heat until melted and smooth, stirring occasionally. Remove from heat. Beat in eggs, sugar, vanilla, and salt until blended. Stir in flour, blending well. Spread evenly in bottom of greased baking pan. Bake 25-30 minutes. Brownies should be moist. Do not overbake. Cool in pan.

Prepare the Chocolate-Marshmallow Frosting. In a medium saucepan, combine chocolate and butter. Heat over low heat until melted and smooth, stirring occasionally. Remove from heat. Add eggs, vanilla, and powdered sugar, beating until smooth. Stir in marshmallows.

While frosting is slightly warm, spread the brownies with frosting. Refrigerate several hours or overnight. Cut chilled brownies into bars. Store in refrigerator.

Turon

Janel Doloiras

Turon is the best, and it's easy to make. You can have it on its own or with ice cream for a delicious dessert. Turon is basically a ripe plantain egg roll. You can add jackfruit if it's available. Some people use regular bananas, but I'm not a big fan of that route.

Ingredients	Directions
ripe plantains	Slice the plantain into pieces that are about 3-4 inches long and about ½ thick. Roll in brown sugar.
jackfruit if you have it (canned is fine) – thinly sliced	Lay a sheet of egg roll wrapper in front of you, point down. Place the plantain on the wrapper about halfway between the midpoints and the bottom point (the point closest to you). If you have jackfruit, you can put a few thin slices on top of the plantain.
egg roll wrappers	Wrap with egg roll wrapper.
whisked egg to seal wrapper	Use whisked egg to seal wrapper.
brown sugar	Toss the egg roll in brown sugar.
oil to fry	Fry until golden brown. The sugar on the outside should caramelize.

Tips:

Egg roll wrappers are thin, so be careful peeling them apart. I would keep most of them in the bag rather than pulling a whole bunch out at a time, so they don't dry out. Make sure to keep the ones you do have out covered with a wet napkin or cloth. Wrap like you would a burrito, first over, then tuck in the sides, and then continue to roll. A tighter roll is always better, but keep in mind that the wrappers are thin and rip easily.

Pistachio Cake

Billie Jo Simmons

Ingredients

1 box white cake mix

2 packages pistachio pudding

1 cup club soda

4 eggs

½ cup oil

powdered sugar

Directions

Preheat oven to 350°F.

Combine the cake mix, eggs, and oil. Mix.

Add the pistachio pudding and club soda. Be careful not to overmix.

Pour into a greased baking dish and bake for 30-45 minutes.

Cool completely, then sprinkle with powdered sugar and enjoy!

"Recovery is something you have to work on every single day, and it's something that doesn't get a day off."

Demi Lovato

Breakfast

"What nicer thing can you do for somebody than make them breakfast?"

Anthony Bourdain

Chocolate Chip Pancakes

Lamar Stevens

I like to cook pancakes with chocolate chips on Christmas Day for my family. It makes me feel good because it reminds me of when I was a kid with my parents and family. Being sober makes it "priceless."

Ingredients

1 ¼ cups flour

1 Tbsp sugar

1 Tbsp baking powder

¼ tsp salt

2 eggs

1 cup milk

4 Tbsp melted butter

1 tsp vanilla

⅓ cup chocolate chips

Directions

Preheat a frying pan or griddle. Add a teaspoon of butter or oil to the pan.

Combine flour, sugar, baking powder, and salt in a large bowl.

Mix together eggs, milk, butter, and vanilla and pour into the dry mixture, mixing until smooth.

Fold in the chocolate chips.

Pour ⅛ to ¼ of a cup onto the hot griddle or frying pan.

Flip when top begins to bubble and looks a little dry. Turn and cook until golden brown. Serve hot on Christmas morning with butter and syrup.

Christmas Morning Breakfast Casserole

Marilyn Gardner

Ingredients

8 oz mozzarella cheese, shredded

8 oz cheddar cheese, shredded

8 slices of bacon, cooked until crispy and crumbled

6 eggs

2 cups milk

salt and pepper to taste

sliced bread

Directions

On Christmas Eve, blend together the eggs, milk, salt, and pepper in a large bowl.

Butter a 9x13 inch pan and line the bottom with bread slices.

Cover the bread with cheese and bacon and pour the egg mixture over everything.

Cover and refrigerate overnight.

On Christmas morning, preheat oven to 350°F.

Take the casserole out of the refrigerator. Check to make sure that it does not look too dry. If it looks dry, pour approximately a 1/2 cup of milk evenly over the casserole.

Bake at 350° for 40 to 50 minutes. The casserole will be golden brown on top. Serve with your favorite hot sauce and cinnamon rolls!

Warm-Your-Bones Oatmeal
Harvard Thompson

Ingredients

2 cups of old fashioned oats (not instant, not steel-cut)

1-1½ cups of whole milk

2 tsp of cinnamon

1 tsp (or more) of authentic maple syrup

a dash of black pepper

optional: a dash of cayenne pepper (for heat)

Directions

Choose your favorite bowl — one that brings you joy.

Pour the oats into the bowl.

Add cinnamon and other spices.

Add maple syrup.

Add milk, but do not stir.

Microwave for 2 minutes. Watch it to make sure it doesn't boil over.

When the milk is absorbed, then it is ready.

Before serving, stir the flavors together.

"I'm not telling you it is going to be easy, I'm telling you it's going to be worth it."

Anonymous

Everything Must Go Omelet

Harvard Thompson

Ingredients

12 eggs (12 eggs will feed 4-6 people)

1-3 bell peppers, diced small

1 small crown broccoli, chopped into small pieces

4-6 mushrooms, thinly sliced

spices (garlic powder, salt, pepper, oregano, red pepper flakes)

your favorite cheese (provolone, cheddar, American, etc)

butter or olive oil for cooking the omelette in the pan

2-3 Tbsp olive oil for cooking vegetables

Directions

In a pan, cook the peppers, broccoli, and mushrooms in olive oil, until tender and slightly brown. Add butter (or more olive oil) to the pan.

Turn heat to medium-high.

In a separate bowl, crack the eggs and whip until frothy with a whisk.

Add the eggs to the pan with cooked vegetables.

Let sit for 2-3 minutes, before using a spatula to maneuver the sides of the omelette (by adjusting the sides, the liquid will spill onto the pan, which helps make the omelette fluffier).

When all liquid has solidified, add spices and cheese.

Using a spatula, fold the omelette in half and let sit for 2 minutes.

Then, carefully flip the entire omelette and brown the other side for 2 minutes. (This step can be skipped if the omelette is not easily moved without disintegrating.) A trick to make this easier is to cover the pan for 2 additional minutes to ensure the inside is cooked.

When ready, portion according to audience, plate, and enjoy with some toast, roasted potatoes, or just as is!

Chocolate Chip Banana Bread

Kylie Brewer

When I was little, I would sleep over at my Nonna's house, and we would make this chocolate chip banana bread together. My siblings and I used to spend every other Saturday night there because my mom had to take overnight weekend shifts as part of her job. We would make it after dinner, have a piece for dessert, and eat it again for breakfast in the morning! My Nonna inspired my love for cooking, and I have so many beloved recipes from her, but this one will always be my favorite.

Ingredients

2 cups all-purpose flour

1 tsp baking soda

¾ cup granulated sugar

¼ brown sugar

½ cup butter, softened

2 eggs - room temperature

¼ cup buttermilk or sour cream

1 tsp vanilla extract

2-3 overripe bananas

optional: 2 cups chocolate chips or walnuts

Directions

Preheat oven to 350°F and grease a bread pan; set aside for later.

In a large bowl, cream together the butter, eggs, and buttermilk or sour cream until smooth.

Add in the brown and granulated sugars slowly and mix until well incorporated.

In a separate small bowl, use a fork to mash the bananas well and add the vanilla extract.

Add the mashed bananas to the butter and sugar mixture. Mix together well.

Combine the baking soda and flour. Add slowly until all the flour has been added. Be very careful not to overmix. Optional: Fold in half the chocolate chips.

Pour bread mix into prepared pan and top with remaining chips (or nuts).

Bake for 55-65 minutes, or until a toothpick can be inserted into the center and removed clean.

Food Resources

I am not defined by my relapses, but by my decision to remain in recovery despite them."

Anonymous

As we think about cooking as a recovery activity, it is also important to acknowledge that food insecurity is a difficult problem in many households. The U.S. Department of Agriculture (USDA) defines food insecurity as a lack of consistent access to enough food for an active, healthy life.[1]

We have included the following community resources to help those who are struggling. Please note that this list is specific to the Fall River, MA, area and can change over time. For up-to-date resources in other areas, visit: freefood.org.

---

[1]   https://www.ers.usda.gov/topics/food-nutrition-assistance/food-security-in-the-u-s/definitions-of-food-security/

Fall River

Feed My Sheep Food Pantry - Fall River, MA
65 Middle St
Fall River, MA, 02720
Phone: (774) 644-7142

Gates Of Hope
112 Flint Street
Fall River, MA, 02723
Phone: (508) 837-1962

Veteran's Assoc. of Bristol County
755 Pine Street
Fall River, MA, 02720
Phone: (508) 679-9277

St Anne's Parish Food Pantry
818 Middle Street
Fall River, MA, 02721
Phone: (508) 674-5651

Salvation Army Fall River Food Assistance
290 Bedford Street
Fall River, MA, 02722
Phone: (508) 679-7900

Sacred Heart Pantry
160 Seabury Street
Fall River, MA, 02720
Phone: (508) 673-0852

Citizens for Citizens Food Pantry
822 Eastern Ave
Fall River, MA, 02720
Phone: (508) 679-0041

Surrounding Area

Annelle Delorme Hagerman Food Pantry
2112 County Street
Somerset, MA, 02726
Phone: (508) 678-9663

Bethany Gospel Chapel
62 Lindsay Lane
Swansea, MA, 02777
Phone: (774) 644-1551

St Mary of the Bay Food Pantry - Warren
645 Main Street
Warren, RI, 02885
Phone: (401) 245-7000

East Bay Community Action Program Tiverton Pantry
1048 Stafford Road
Tiverton, RI, 02878
Phone: (401) 625-5134

Tap-In Barrington Food Pantry
281 County Road
Barrington, RI, 02806
Phone: (401) 247-1444

East Bay Food Pantry
532 Wood St
Bristol, RI, 02809
Phone: (401) 396-9490

Index